PATH OF TOTAL

THE TOTAL SOLAR ECLIPSE
OF AUGUST 21, 2017

MAINE

VERMONT

NEW HAMPSHIRE

NNESOTA

WISCONSIN

MICHIGAN

NEW YORK

MASSACHUSETTS
RHODE ISLAND
CONNECTICUT

IOWA

PENNSYLVANIA

NEW JERSEY

ILLINOIS

OHIO

MARYLAND

DELAWARE

INDIANA

WEST
VIRGINIA

VIRGINIA

1:15 P.M. CENTRAL DAYLIGHT TIME

KENTUCKY

MISSOURI

NORTH CAROLINA

TENNESSEE

SOUTH CAROLINA

ARKANSAS

2:45 P.M. EASTERN DAYLIGHT TIME

MISSISSIPPI

GEORGIA

ALABAMA

LOUISIANA

FLORIDA

P S E

ANDY
RASH

SCHOLASTIC PRESS · NEW YORK

Two months ago, I learned there would be a total solar eclipse. The Sun would go completely behind the Moon and the Moon would cast a shadow on Earth! But to see it happen, I would have to be in the right place at the right time.

I decided to make a plan.

A month ago, I picked out the perfect place and time to watch the eclipse. At this location on the path of totality, the Moon will be totally blocking the Sun's light for two minutes and forty seconds! Dad said we could drive there.

PATH OF TOTALITY

A week ago, I ordered special dark glasses to protect our eyes when we watch the eclipse. Staring right at the Sun would damage our eyes, so wearing official eclipse glasses is important.

But first, I tried them out.

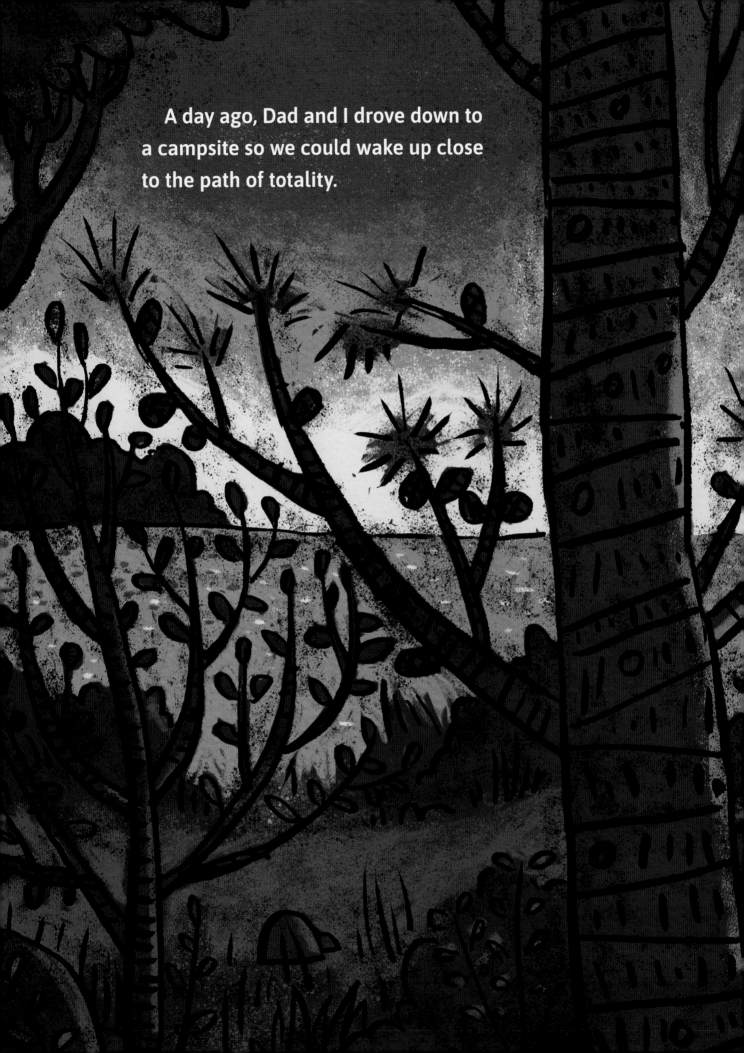

A day ago, Dad and I drove down to a campsite so we could wake up close to the path of totality.

An hour ago, we packed up our stuff to get to the spot I picked out.

A minute ago, the Sun began to hide
behind the Moon. We barely made it!

A second ago, the Sun disappeared
behind the Moon.

Now, Dad and I are in the dark.

We take off our special glasses. Sunset colors glow all around.
Crickets chirp. Dogs bark. Streetlights turn on. They all think
it's nighttime!

Shimmering rays shine around the Moon. I try not to blink.
We are in the perfect place at the perfect time.

A second from now, the Sun will burst out from behind the Moon. We'll put our special glasses back on. It will be time to go.

A minute from now, we will see crescent-moon-shaped spots of sunlight on the ground as we walk back to the car.

An hour from now, we'll be stuck in a big traffic jam going home.

I'll be sad the eclipse is over.

A day from now, I'll close my eyes and try to remember everything. I'll find out when the next eclipse will happen in the United States: not for years.

A year from now, Dad and I will still talk about what we saw.
We won't remember everything, but it will be fun to try.

Years from now, we'll go again. And once more,
we'll be in the perfect place at the perfect time.

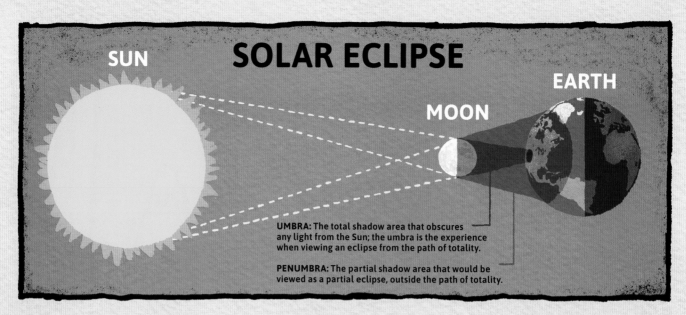

SOLAR ECLIPSE

SUN

MOON

EARTH

UMBRA: The total shadow area that obscures any light from the Sun; the umbra is the experience when viewing an eclipse from the path of totality.

PENUMBRA: The partial shadow area that would be viewed as a partial eclipse, outside the path of totality.

When the Moon blocks some or all of the Sun from our view here on Earth, it is called a SOLAR ECLIPSE. There are three main types of solar eclipses.

TOTAL ECLIPSE
The Moon completely blocks the Sun from our view, allowing us to see the outermost part of the Sun's atmosphere, called the CORONA.

ANNULAR ECLIPSE
The Moon is too far away from Earth to completely block the Sun. The uncovered area of the Sun forms a bright ring around the Moon, often called a ring of fire.

PARTIAL ECLIPSE
The Moon blocks part of the Sun but is not centered from our viewpoint.

FINDING THE PATH
Scientists use math to predict when and where on Earth eclipses will be visible. The Moon's shadow makes a different path for each eclipse. The PATH OF TOTALITY is where a total eclipse can be seen, and the PATH OF ANNULARITY is where an annular eclipse can be seen.

ECLIPSE GLASSES
It is dangerous to stare at the Sun, and regular sunglasses aren't strong enough to protect your eyes. To view a solar eclipse, get ISO-approved glasses (ISO stands for International Organization for Standardization). They are so dark that you can't really see anything through them other than the Sun or bright lights. For a total eclipse, you can take them off briefly to view the Sun's corona, but put them back on when the Sun peeks out on the other side of the Moon.

A NOTE FROM THE AUTHOR

This book is based on a trip I took with my son to watch the solar eclipse on August 21, 2017. We traveled from our home in Wisconsin to Golconda, Illinois, the place closest to us on the path of totality.

During the eclipse, we were surprised by many things, including the immediate sound of crickets, the astonishing view of the Sun's corona, and the crescent-shaped dappling of sunlight on the ground.

If you can go — do it! It's worth it. But if you can't, just remember that there are all kinds of amazing experiences to have as long as you're with the people you love.

For Joe

All rights reserved. Published by Scholastic Press, an imprint of Scholastic Inc., *Publishers since 1920.* SCHOLASTIC, SCHOLASTIC PRESS, and associated logos are trademarks and/or registered trademarks of Scholastic Inc.

Library of Congress Cataloging-in-Publication Data available

ISBN 978-1-338-60882-3

10 9 8 7 6 5 4 3 2 1   23 24 25 26 27

Printed in China   38
First edition, September 2023

A NOTE ABOUT THE MAPS: The map at the front of this book shows the path of the Moon's shadow as it moved across the United States on August 21, 2017, during the total eclipse. The map at the back of this book shows the paths the Moon's shadow will take across the United States during total eclipses and annular eclipses for the next twenty-five years. The maps in this book were created from information on the website greatamericaneclipse.com.

Many thanks to Jacqueline Faherty, Senior Scientist, Department of Astrophysics, American Museum of Natural History.

Book design by Andy Rash and Charles Kreloff
The artwork in this book was created digitally, incorporating textures and elements painted with gouache on watercolor paper.

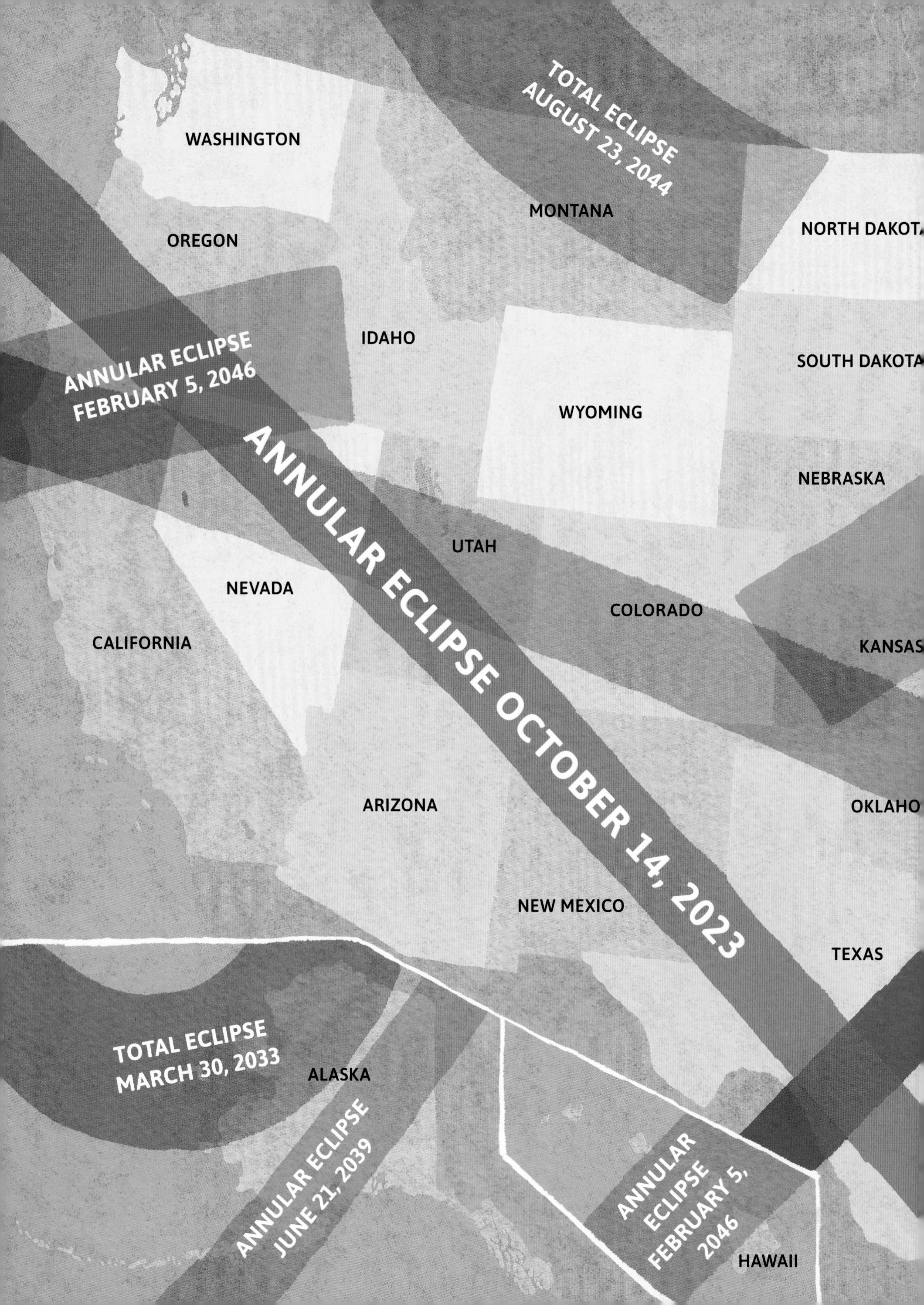

WASHINGTON
TOTAL ECLIPSE AUGUST 23, 2044
MONTANA
NORTH DAKOTA
OREGON
IDAHO
SOUTH DAKOTA
ANNULAR ECLIPSE FEBRUARY 5, 2046
WYOMING
ANNULAR ECLIPSE OCTOBER 14, 2023
NEBRASKA
UTAH
NEVADA
COLORADO
CALIFORNIA
KANSAS
ARIZONA
OKLAHOMA
NEW MEXICO
TEXAS
TOTAL ECLIPSE MARCH 30, 2033
ALASKA
ANNULAR ECLIPSE JUNE 21, 2039
ANNULAR ECLIPSE FEBRUARY 5, 2046
HAWAII